CALM THE FUCK DOWN

A HUMOROUS AND
IRREVERENT
ADULT COLORING
BOOK

COLOR TEST PAGE

COLOR TEST PAGE

SOMETHING
TO DO
UNTIL
KICKS IN

NO

Anything
is
Possible

ALL
you
need
is
LOVE

Love

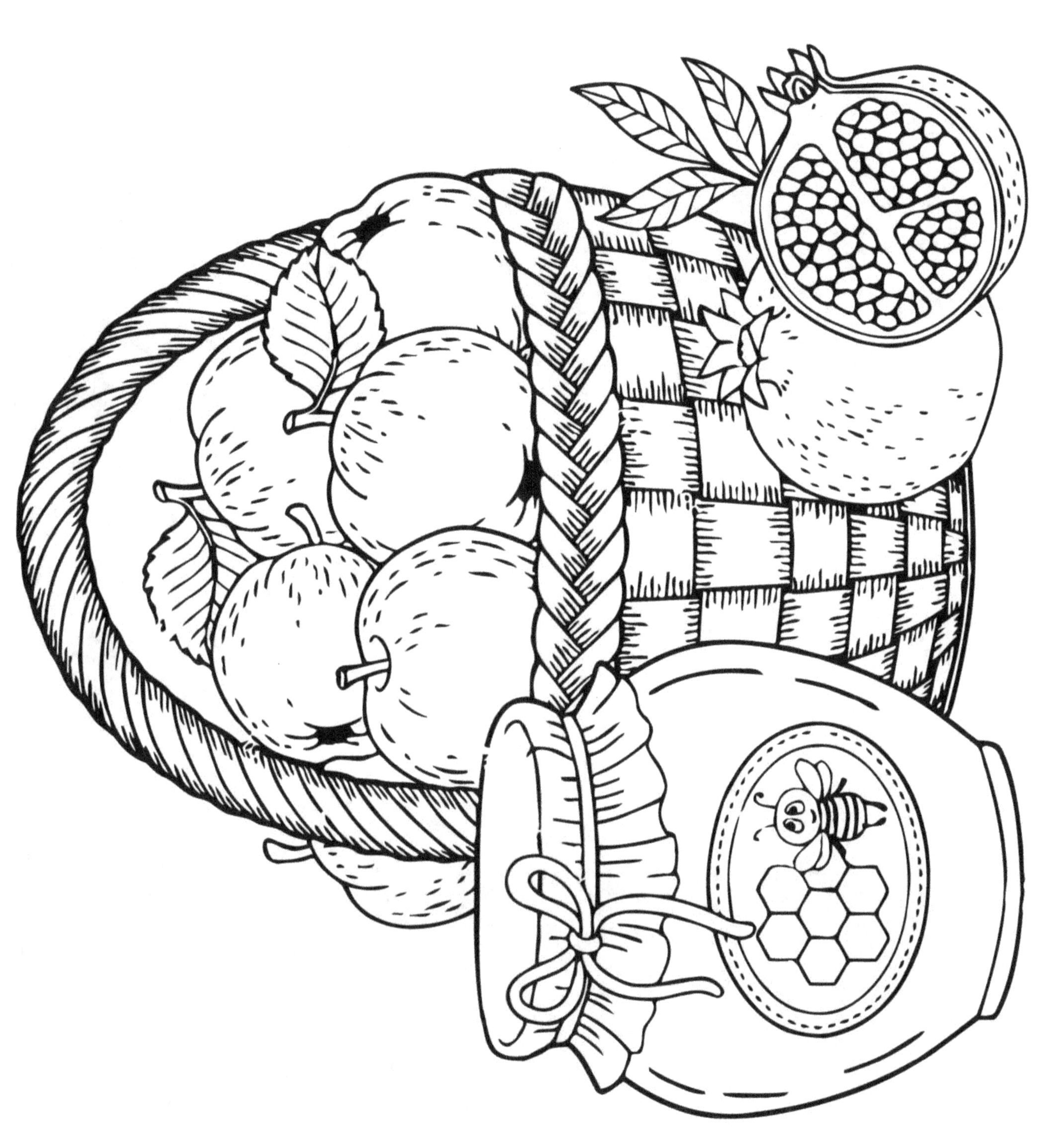

LOVE you

Me
Sarcastic
Never

LOVE

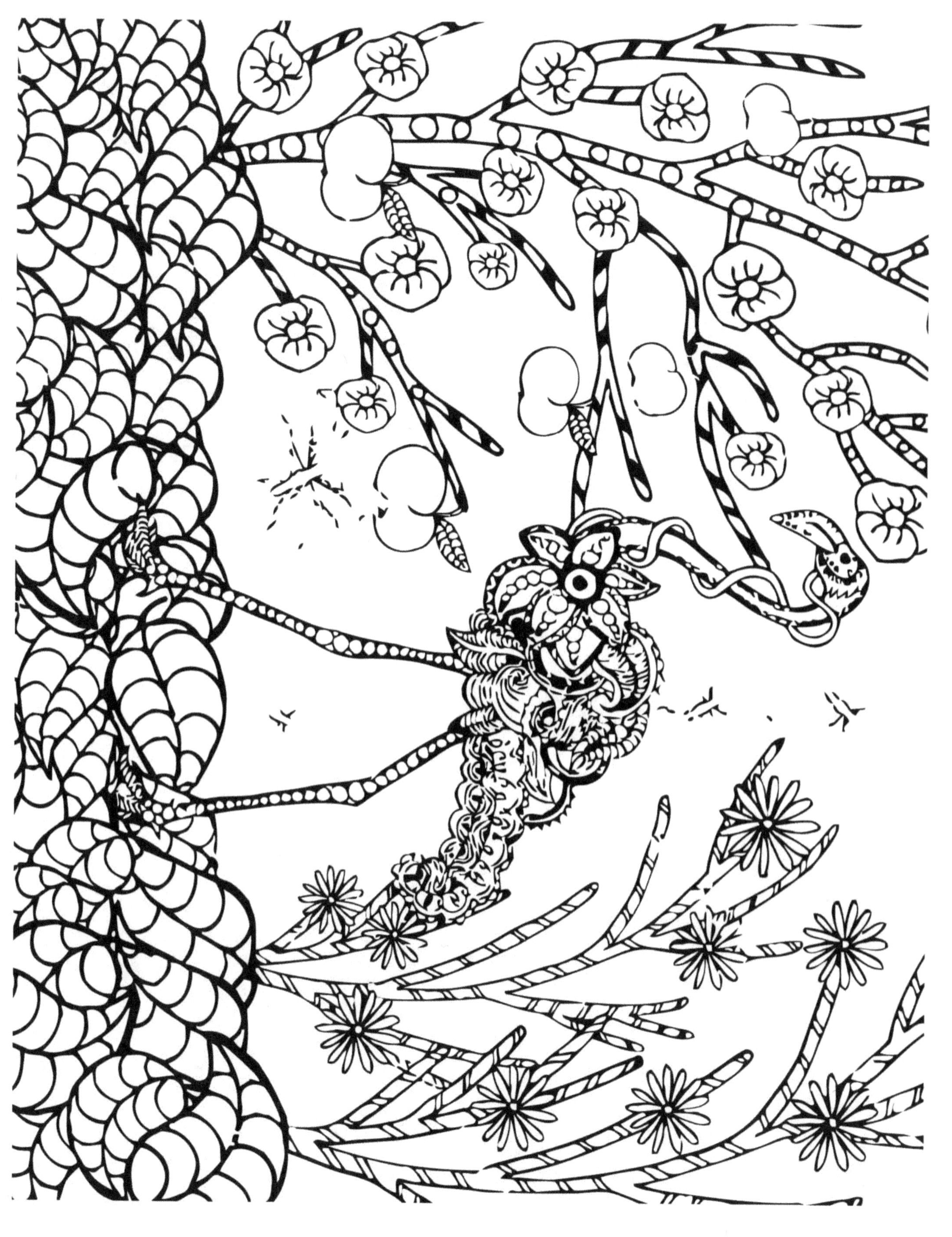

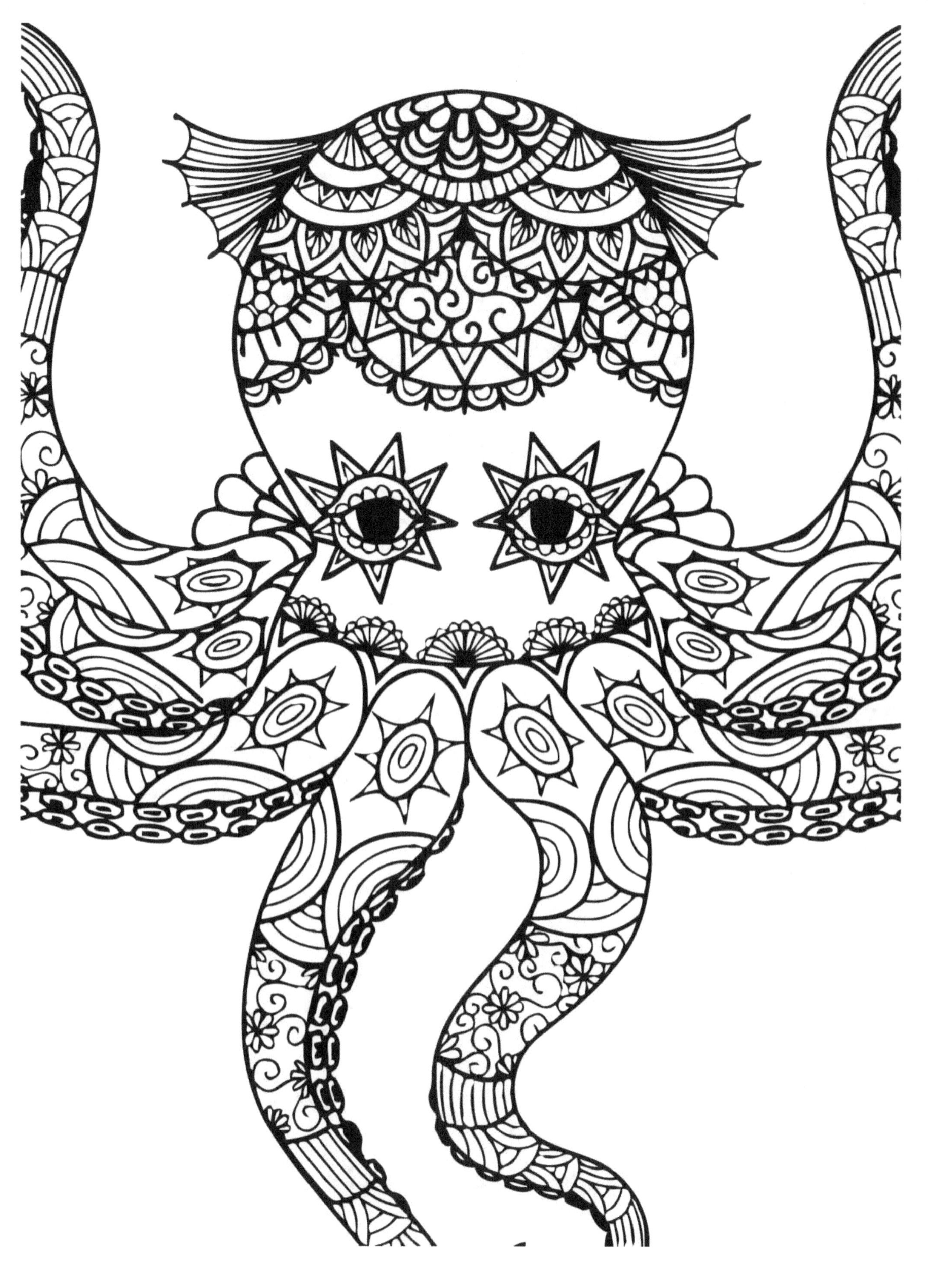

Stay
Strong

HAVE A
NICE
DAY

Thank You